RAMBLINGS OF
AN OLD TEDDY

*Poems and illustrations by
Joan Osborn*

First published in Great Britain in 2009
Reprinted 2016

Text & illustration copyright © 2009 Joan Osborn

Book design by Andrew Buller 2016. Published by Andrew Buller Books.
www.andrewbuller.com

All rights reserved. No part of this publication may be reproduced, stored in a retrieval system, or transmitted, in any form or by any means, electronic, mechanical, photocopying, recording or otherwise, without the prior permission of the copyright owner.

ISBN: 978-1530381210

OLD BEAR BOOKS
www.oldbearbooks.com

**Dedicated to Floss – a dear friend,
without whose nagging this
would never have been written**

**and Rebecca – granddaughter,
without whose computer wizardry
it would never have been presentable**

Half of the proceeds of this book will be donated to the Pilgrims Hospice,
who cared for Joan's husband in his and the family's time of need.
The Pilgrims Hospice is a registered charity (293968) and resides in Thanet,
Ashford and Canterbury.

Contents

Date of Birth	4
The Postman	6
While out Shopping	8
Oh how	10
This is the me	12
Never Let	14
Am I the only one	16
Everyone Shrinks	18
At a Meeting	20
The Mirror	22
Afterlife	24
Remember When	26
A Fact	28
Technology	30
When I was Young	32
Rebecca	34

Date of birth and postcode
Mothers maiden name
Third digit of your security code
What's this - a new quiz game?
No - it's not Chris Tarrant
And I don't want to phone a friend,
I want to talk to a human
Before I go round the bend
Not press two if you want accounts
Press three if you want to pay
Press four if you want to know the amount
Paid into your bank today
I don't want to listen to Mozart
I don't want to hold the line
I don't want thanks for my patience
I want to hear a voice like mine!
A human voice, which says "good day"
And "can I help in any way"

Remember when the postman
In his uniform and hat
Brought the letters twice a day
With a brisk rat a tat tat?
Newsy letters from a friend –
Maybe a card or two,
Greetings and invitations
Especially for you?
I like my current postman
With his cheeky shorts and smile
But when I see him coming
I want to run a mile!
Once a day at lunchtime
The dreaded mail arrives
Brown envelopes and Tax returns –
The bane of all our lives.
Complicated letters and bills
I really don't understand
Advertisements and questionnaires
On the doormat land.
This one's for the rubbish,
This one I must pay
This one I can't understand –
I'll ask my son one day.

There should be a course
For old Biddies like me
To cope with the mail we receive
And then we'd welcome the postman
And not wish he would leave!

While out shopping the other day
I saw an old lady heading my way
She must be really old I thought
And look at the load of shopping she's bought
I think I'd better help her out
She'd be really grateful I'd no doubt
So I bent to put my own bags down
And when I straightened with a frown
I realized - and was shocked to see
No little old lady, but a reflection of me!

Oh how I'd love a relaxing bath
To comfort my poor old bones.
And how I'd like to get in it
Without the moans and groans.
I'd be so proud that I'd got in
With lather and bubbles
Up to my chin
But after the pride, comes the doubt
O K I got in - but can I get out?
I've done some thinking about it
And the answer is I doubt it!
I've tried before to no avail
And I always end up
Like an old beached whale!

This is the me that no one can see
I look and I feel a wreck!
I don't understand,
I hadn't quite planned
To sound such a pain in the neck!
Think that you can and you will
I've been told
Is the way to cope with getting old?
But thinking is the difficult part
To believe that you can
With your head and your heart.
So shower away the sleep of the night,
Pull up your socks with all your might
Face the new day - it's nearly nine
And if anyone asks, say "I FEEL FINE"!

Never let an inanimate object
Know you're in a hurry
Never let the thing suspect
Or see you're in a flurry
A nail that bends when hammered,
A screw which just won't screw
A kit which won't be assembled
Or a joint which just won't glue
A needle with an eye too small
But the point sticks into your skin
The key which refuses to open the lock
When you only want to get in!
Whatever it is that's defiant
Will respond and be compliant if -
You travel on an even keel,
Pretend that all is calm
Never let the object feel
You'll do it any harm
If - after all this it refuses
To do just as you say
Don't blow all your fuses,
Throw the bloody thing away.

Am I the only one who finds
And am I the only one who minds
That when we sit and watch T V
We must keep the zapper on our knee?
Do you strain your ears to hear
A really touching scene?
Then have to turn the volume down
When the "Ads" come in between?
Do advertisers pay extra
For the sound to be so high?
Or think if they blast us out of our chairs
We'll all go out and buy?
Quite the reverse applies to me
With the zapper at the ready on my knee
I know I can be a perverse old bat
But I will not buy if I'm shouted at -
Gentle persuasion's the way to go
Please let the advertisers know!

Everyone shrinks
When they're older they say
So why is the floor getting further away
I think I'm getting taller
No one has moved the floor
And then I find I stretch to reach
The top shelf at the store!
Perhaps sometimes we're small
When we want to reach up high
And taller at another time
Although I can't think why.
Can't work it out,
Can't think any more
I know what to blame -
I blame Sod's law!

At a meeting of designers
They agreed to have some fun
And design a lot of products
That just can't be undone!
Yes, they'll look attractive
As they tempt us at the store
But when we try to open them
They end up on the floor!
Bottles with caps, which we have to learn
The intricate way to twist and turn
Immovable lids on beetroot jars
Untearable foil on chocolate bars,
Tremendous fun for designer's maybe
But oh! So annoying for you and me

I glimpsed a sight in the mirror
No one would like to see
What is this apparition looking back at me?
Unwashed, uncombed and lazy
Thank God the mirror's hazy,
If this thing appeared in the dead of night
It'd give Beelzebub a fright!
Really can't believe it's me
And if it is I don't want to see!
Pull down the blind - dim the light-
Don't want to see this awful sight.
I'll take a shower - do my hair
A bit of make up and if I dare
Look again, and maybe see
This new reflection's really me!

I'm not sure I believe in an afterlife,
Though I know I really should
So, just in case there is one,
I'm trying to be good.
I try to keep a shoulder,
On which my friends can cry,
I keep the kettle boiling
For neighbours calling by.
I can't pretend I'm an angel,
I've done my share of wrong
And I'm nowhere the category
To which the saints belong,
But if there's a Heaven and if there's a Hell
Where I want to go I know quite well.
I love the winter weather,
Feel ill when the temperature's high
So may I go to Heaven please?
If I go to Hell I'll die!

Remember when, as children
Regardless of the miles
We marched from school
To the Parish Church in endless crocodiles?
One teacher at the head of us
Another at the back
And if we misbehaved ourselves
We'd sometimes get a smack.
"Straighten your backs – Don't drag your feet
Hold your heads up high
Create a good impression
To the people passing by"
Marching across the High Street
Prayer books in our hand
And if it was a Saint's day, preceded by a band!
I think it was planned to encourage us
To go to church and pray
To lead a good clean Christian life
And never go astray
But for us it was just a day off
From reading and writing and sums
And after the boring service
Home early to our Mums!

A fact I've noticed recently
Is that people are talking more quietly
Wish they'd speak up without delay
Cos I don't hear a word they say
I might miss a bit of gossip
Or a little bit of spice
And I feel such an idiot
If they have to say it twice.
I've noticed too, my neighbours-
Who always scrap and row
Must be getting on better
Cos I hardly hear them now
My alarm clock doesn't wake me
However long it rings
My doorbell's getting quieter
And lots of other things.
You think I'm getting deaf you say
But can that really be?
Think I'll forget all about it
And make a cup of tea

In this age of technology –
The computer and the jet
I thought I'd list the things we've lost
Before we all forget
The man at the bank who's name we knew
And could ask for a bit of advice
Tradesmen arriving the day they're due
Not having to phone them twice
The village post office and general store
Where we could meet and have a jaw
The policeman plodding around his beat
Going home with tired feet
A chat with a neighbour over the fence
L S D meant pounds shillings and pence
A gentle stroll down a country lane
Ice inside the window pane
A game of cricket in the street –
No parked cars in the way
Crumpets toasted by the fire
At the end of a busy day
Children's hour and Uncle Mac,
Monday night at eight
Sunday tea at Grandmas
With winkles on the plate

Going home - feed the ducks in the park
See the lamp lighter
Lighting the lamps in the dark.
The zinc bath filled from the copper
In front of the Kitchener fire
The crackly sound of the wireless
Which I always thought had a wire
I could go on for page after page
Evoking memories for people my age -
So I'll put my rose coloured glasses away
And settle down to another day
In my cosy centrally heated house
With my computer and my trusty mouse!

To Tom and Lucy

A long time ago when I was young
I remember how our heads we hung
When my Mother no matter
How sweet would say
Time to put those toys away
Today is thank you letter day!
Preparations all were made,
Pens and paper on the table laid
And my brothers and I would sit and moan
Why a letter, can't we phone?
If I'd known then what a joy it is
To receive a thank you letter
I'd have written mine
With much more grace
And made my writing better.
I appreciate the cards you wrote
And so I send this little note
To say Thank you!

I feel guilty and extremely bad
Cos I've nearly sent Rebecca mad
By taking up her precious time
Helping me with a book of rhyme!
The rhymes and illustrations were all OK
But how could I present them
In a satisfactory way?
I'm a novice on the computer –
Not had it long enough
To be anywhere near proficient
At the complicated stuff.
Rebecca on the other hand –
Really seems to understand
But she says my computer's sensitive
And won't do what it's told
My printer says it's got a queue
It's like me - getting old
But she really has persisted
And got the upper hand
Using a few expletives
Which I don't understand
Everything's in order now
And I owe it all to Bec
And just by way of a thank you
I'm sending a little cheque!

Joan Osborn, born in Bromley in 1929, is affectionately known as "Bear" by her close friends and family. She has been a keen golfer, artist, potter, poet, guest house keeper, foster parent, wife and full-time mum.

She lives in a pretty cottage in Broadstairs, Kent and keeps busy with her growing family and beloved garden. She spends more on feeding the birds than herself!

Half of the proceeds of this book will be donated to the Pilgrims Hospice, who cared for Joan's husband in his and the family's time of need. The Pilgrims Hospice is a registered charity (293968) and resides in Thanet, Ashford and Canterbury.

OLD BEAR BOOKS
www.oldbearbooks.com

Printed in Great Britain
by Amazon